AF604220

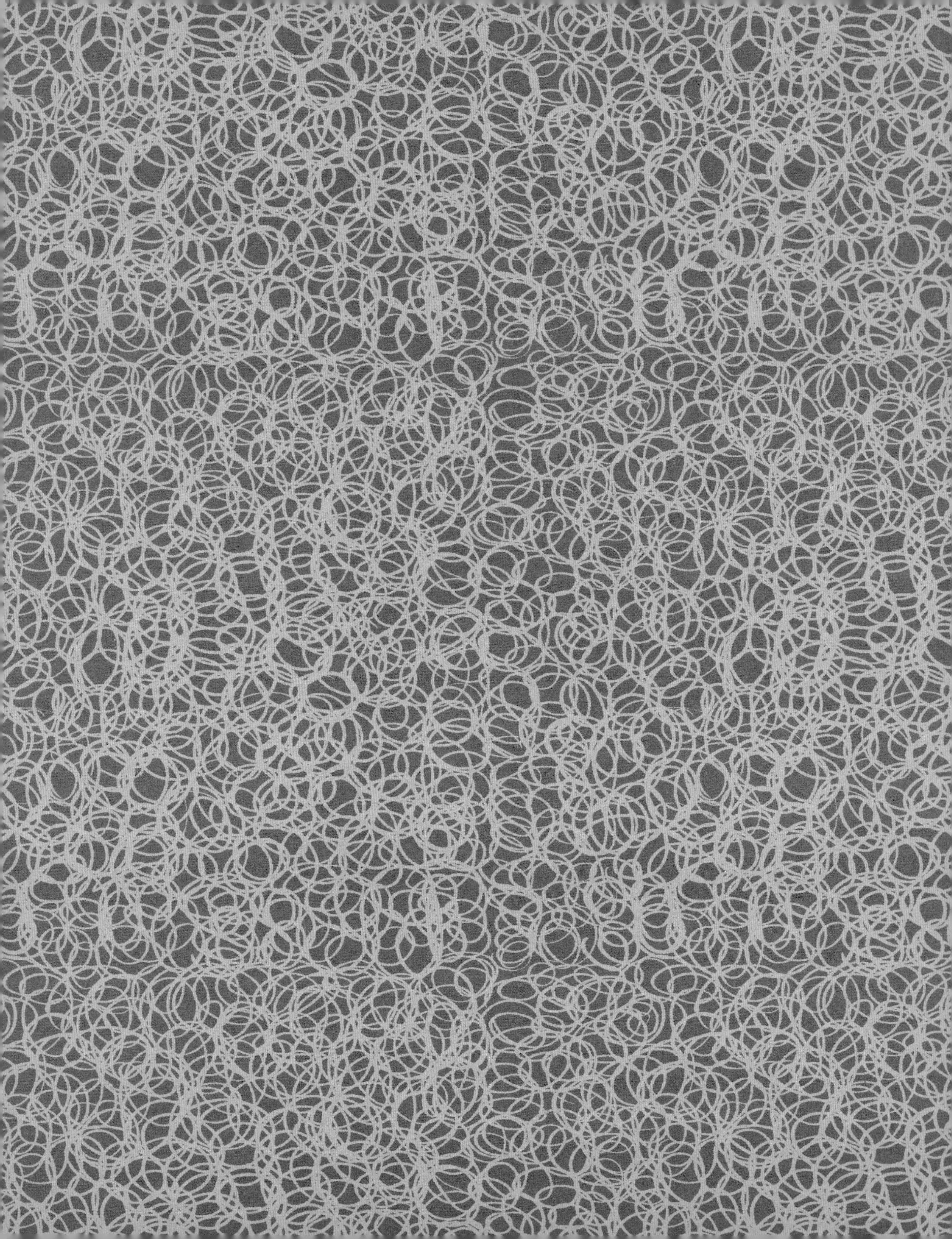

Imagination

written by
Zanni Louise
art by
Missy Turner

FIVE MILE

Hi, I am Jack.
My name
is Lila!
Hola, I am Mina.

I am Li Wei.
I'm Rosie ...
... and this is Freckles!

A big heart helps you care for the world, care for yourself, and care for others.

But how do you grow your heart?

One ingredient you can use to grow your heart is imagination.

What is imagination?
There are many ways
to be imaginative ...

Imagination is creating something out of nothing. As long as you pack your imagination, you'll never be bored!

Mina's family goes to the beach.

Her sister, Juniper, is reading.
Her mums are busy chatting.
Mina wishes she had at least
brought a bucket and spade.

But then Mina's imagination carries her away to a magical place.

The piece of driftwood makes the perfect mast for her pirate ship.
And seaweed makes the sails!

Mina spends the afternoon zooming across the high seas, finding treasure on Robber Island, and rescuing a mermaid!

Imagination helps you solve problems.

It's Book Week. And Jack is the only kid without a costume.

He's disappointed, because he loves dressing up.

But then he uses his imagination. Jack makes glasses using his sandwich wrapper. His pencil is a wand. And Lila draws a lightning bolt down Jack's forehead.

Jack is a boy wizard from his favourite book, and puts spells on all the other kids!

Imagination helps you learn about each other and understand each other.

There is a new girl on Lila's bus.

When the girl moves seats, Lila's heart crumples.

Lila tries to imagine why the girl was unkind.

Is she shy? wonders Lila. Maybe she just wants to be alone.

Lila knows when she has big feelings, she likes being alone too.

Lila watches the girl draw clouds in the window.

Imagining how the other girl feels helps Lila feel better.

You can use your imagination to wonder about how the world works.

'Dad, why does the moon glow?' Rosie asks.

'Maybe the man on the moon has a lantern,' jokes Dad.

'Or a light switch!' says Rosie.

Rosie has never been to the moon, so she can't know for sure. But she lets her mind scurry about.

'Maybe the sun shines on the moon, and that makes it glow,' says Rosie.

You can imagine new ways to make a better world.

Jack is worried about how much petrol the school bus uses. His school has solar panels on its roof. So does his house.

Why can't the bus use the sun's energy to drive? wonders Jack.

He draws the school bus, with solar panels on its roof. He adds a garden too, just for fun.

Jack imagines solar-powered garden-growing buses driving around the world!

One day, Jack's dreams might become reality!

Imagination gives you a place to escape when things are tricky. And the freedom to be who you want to be.

When Li Wei isn't picked for the soccer team, he kicks the tree trunk.

But then he pulls his hat over his eyes, takes long breaths, and disappears into a place where he feels calm.

It's just Li Wei and Sandy, playing together in the long grass. He can hear the stream. And smell the jasmine.

In this place, Li Wei is the best soccer player in the world!

Imagination helps you try new things.

The kayak bobs in the water.

Mina has never been on a kayak before.

What if she sinks?
What if she can't paddle?

But then Mina closes her eyes. She imagines herself stepping into the kayak and paddling down the river.

Her arms are strong.
Her kayak is fast!

Mina opens her eyes, takes a big breath and climbs into the kayak.

Imagination can make ordinary things magic.

It's Clean-Up Day at Lila's house.
Lila grumbles. She hates cleaning.

But Rosie is smiling. 'Beeeep!
He-llo Li-la. I am Ro-bot Ro-sie.
I must clean up Mars!'

‘Oh yeah! Let’s clean up before the astronauts arrive!’ says Lila.

‘Beep beep ... ew!’ says Rosie, picking up a dirty sock. ‘These aliens are ve-ry mess-y!’

Lila giggles. She pulls on her planet-cleaning gloves, and helps Robot Rosie tidy up after messy aliens!

Imagination brings friends together, through stories.

Mina, Jack, Li Wei, Rosie and Lila are cloud watching.

'The robot is captain of the spaceship!' says Rosie, as a spaceship cloud forms in the sky.

'Wait! Isn't that a wizard?' says Jack, pointing.

'That's not a spaceship. It's a pirate ship!' says Mina.

The cloud stories become star stories.

Later, the friends tell each other ghost stories, huddled under the quilt.

Imagination brings friends together. It helps you understand how others might think or feel, so you know how to respond.

Imagination helps you learn about the world,

and create solutions for the future.

It also gives you the freedom to explore who you want to be.

Anything is possible, when you use your imagination.

Imagination helps your heart grow,
so you can look after the world,
yourself and each other.

Can you think of ways you use your imagination?

Let's talk about imagination

What role does imagination play in your life?

John principal

'I always imagine big things. That is what drives me. When creating the Living School, I envision our future. I can 'see' what needs to be done to make people wonder ... to become wonder-full. Imagination is the sweet plaything of my industry. Imagination makes me feel real.'

Jenny playwright

'I created a play about two kids trapped inside a video game. I had to imagine the whole world of the game and make up all the tasks. We used sounds and music to help the audience believe it was actually happening.'

Tiff environmental educator

'I believe our imagination is our greatest gift and tool. It allows us to explore the past, the vast beautiful world beyond, and imagine our way forward into the bright future. Our imagination is our key tool for problem solving and creatively imagining our way forward.'

Tristan author for kids and teens

'My mum told me that 99% of actors were out of work. I didn't listen to her. It takes a big leap to trust your imagination and creativity, but I've spent my life acting, TV presenting, writing scripts and children's books. You just have to combine imagination with really hard work!'

Discussion questions for children

Our imagination can help us solve problems, deal with feelings or just have more fun. There are lots of ways to use our imagination. We can tell stories, draw, paint, sing, dance, build things, explore nature or visit other places in our minds.

- Have you played a game that required you to use your imagination? Tell me about it.
- What task do you have to do that is a bit boring? Now let's use our imagination to make that job more fun.
- Is there a problem you would like to solve? Let's use our imagination to think of some ways to solve this problem.
- Is there somewhere you'd like to go that you've never been? Let's close our eyes and go there now. What can you see? What can you hear?

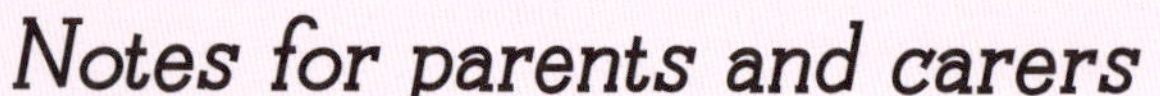

Notes for parents and carers

Imagination is an important part of a child's social, emotional and cognitive development, and can be nurtured in children of all abilities. Imagination helps children make sense of the world. It helps them satisfy their curiosity, challenge themselves, solve problems and express their feelings.

Children use their imagination from a young age, often through imaginative, or 'pretend', play. They might imitate others, play the role of a fantasy character, create an imaginary friend or act out their own stories. They might use everyday objects to represent something different or to build something new. Imaginative play helps children manage their emotions, understand the feelings of others and consider different perspectives. It also helps them stay focussed and persevere with difficult or repetitive tasks.

It is important to encourage imagination as children grow, so they can deal with challenges, connect with others and contribute to the world in positive and creative ways.

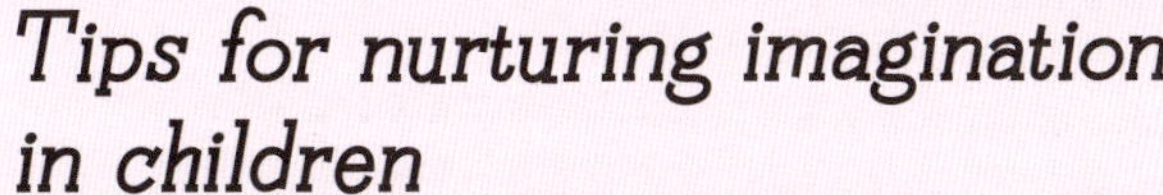

Tips for nurturing imagination in children

- Provide your child with lots of opportunities for unstructured play. Give them open-ended materials like puppets, dress-ups, clay, building blocks, pencils, paints and musical instruments. Set limits around screen time and encourage them to play outdoors using their bodies, senses and natural objects like twigs, leaves, water and sand. Allow your child to feel bored sometimes and simply let their imagination wander.
- Nurture imagination through storytelling. When reading books together, ask questions about how the characters feel, what might happen next, or how else the story could end. Encourage them to tell their own stories using words, pictures, objects and role-play.
- When your child encounters a problem, allow them to find their own solutions, make mistakes and experiment with different strategies. If they get stuck, they could close their eyes and imagine themselves solving the problem.
- While imagining future possibilities can be helpful, it can sometimes lead to worry. If your child is worried about the future, listen, acknowledge their feelings and encourage them to use their imagination in constructive ways. For each worry, ask them to imagine an outcome that is more positive or realistic. Encourage them to write a story about their worry that has a happy ending. Help them come up with creative solutions to future problems and explore ways to cope with difficult emotions.
- Spend time playing with your child, letting them take the lead and come up with their own ideas. Relax and be present with your child, simply listening, watching and sharing in moments of joy. This special time will build their confidence, strengthen your relationship, and help them feel safe, connected and more creative.

Dr Ameika Johnson Child Clinical Psychologist

Also available in this book series

Honesty

Honesty is talking to yourself and others truthfully.

There are many ways to be honest ...

Persistence

Persistence is never giving up, even when things get tough.

There are many ways to be persistent ...

Courage

Courage is stepping towards things we think are scary or difficult.

There are many ways to be courageous ...

Kindness

Kindness is being generous with our words, our actions and our heart.

There are many ways to be kind ...

Resilience

Resilience is bouncing back from difficult moments.

There are many ways to be resilient ...

Made with love by the team at

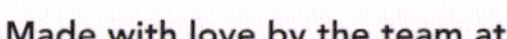

FIVE MILE

Alex, Niki, Rocco, Graham, Jacqui, Claire, Amy, Lyndal, Jessica & Emily

Five Mile,
the publishing division
of Regency Media
www.fivemile.com.au

First published 2021

A catalogue record for this book is available from the National Library of Australia

Printed in China 5 4 3 2

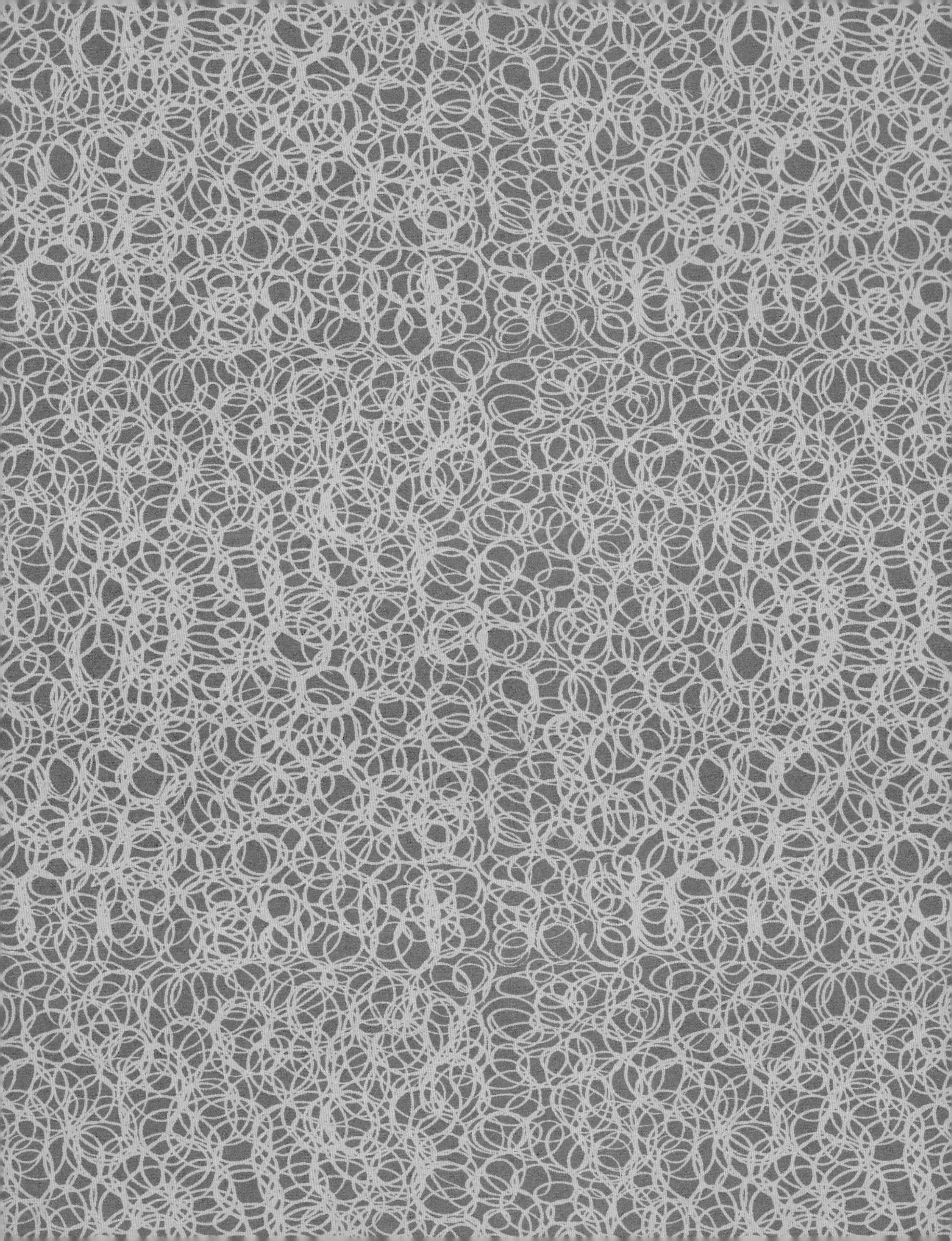